RAILWAYS IN CHESHIRE

THE BUILDING OF
RAILWAYS
IN
CHESHIRE

DOWN TO 1860

By

H. J. Hewitt

Published by
E. J. MORTEN (Publishers)
Didsbury, Manchester, England

First published 1972 by
E. J. MORTEN (PUBLISHER)
Warburton Street, Didsbury,
Manchester, England

H. J. HEWITT   1972

ISBN 0 901598 43 7

Printed in Great Britain by
Scolar Press Limited, Menston, Yorkshire

CONTENTS

LIST OF ILLUSTRATIONS

Chapter One

PARLIAMENT AND THE RAILWAYS

The first railway constructed in Cheshire, the Grand Junction, was promoted without reference to the movement of passengers or goods originating in the county: its purpose was to link Birmingham with Warrington and thence with Liverpool and Manchester. The line ran north through Stafford, entered Cheshire at Wrinehill, 350 feet above sea level, descended to the plain, ran some twenty miles north-north-west, then swung round in a great curve and crossed the Mersey at Lower Walton.

Just as the Grand Junction Railway line reached completion, the London and Birmingham Railway was opened. These two lines used a single station in Birmingham and thus produced a connected system linking the largest towns in England with one another and also with the capital; and as railways developed rapidly northward to Lancaster, to Carlisle and to Glasgow, the backbone of railway communications in the west of England passed through Cheshire. Inevitably this line attracted traffic from both west and east: from Holyhead, Chester and Birkenhead, from Shrewsbury, from the Potteries and (by a shorter route than that mentioned above) from Manchester. At half a dozen places, junctions with the Grand Junction might have been made. Actually one great junction brought the various lines of communication into a single point, and that point was in Cheshire: from Crewe the lines radiated in six directions. It is with the development of the railway system within the county of Cheshire, with the construction of the lines and the effects produced by the early railways that the following pages are concerned.

The late 1820s had seen the construction of several short lines and the Liverpool and Manchester Railway had been opened in 1830. A contemporary who had watched the laying of that line wrote enthusiastically of "a mode of conveyance which for speed, elegance and economy is altogether novel and astonishing", of "formidable obstacles so happily surmounted", of the possibility of "taking a jaunt to Manchester and back before the hours of business in the morning or a like excursion in the evening by way of rest and recreation after the labours of the day". "The husbandman and the careful housewife", he said, might "speedily arrive at their respective marts without enduring the protracted delay and jostling of a market cart", and he went on to instance the transport of coal by rail as a national advantage "for it will lessen the cost of manufacture and commercial transit".

The last prediction of course came true. For some years proposals for railway construction met with powerful opposition both in Parliament and in the country, but manufacturers were quick to see the advantages railway transport offered for the conveyance of coal from the pit to the factory, and of exports from the factory to the seaport, while the speed and comfort of travel by rail were equally evident to the business men. The prosperity of an England already deeply plunged into an age of industry depended on the construction of railways which, in its turn, depended on the enterprise of investors, the skill of civil and mechanical engineers and the willingness of Parliament to grant the necessary facilities.

Though each railway undertaking was unique, the scores of railway companies formed between, say, 1825 and 1845 tended to follow a very similar pattern in origin, in development, in obstacles encountered, and in the work of construction. Railway development in Cheshire was but a local phase of developments occurring in other counties. It had, however, its own logic and for several reasons, it came earlier in Cheshire than in most parts of England.

The general pattern may be stated briefly. A body of men believe that capital could be raised and profitably invested in a railway connecting town X with town Y. They call in a civil engineer. He surveys the country between the two towns, proposes a route, offers a plan and an estimate of the cost of constructing the proposed line. The group invite investors to state the value of the shares they would be prepared to take up. A plan of the proposed route or line is sent to the clerk of the peace in every parish through which the proposed line will pass.

In order that the promoters may have authority to proceed with their project, parliamentary sanction must be obtained. A parliamentary agent is engaged. He is furnished with every relevant detail of the proposals, including the names, occupations, places of residence and proposed holdings of the "proprietors", together with the "assents", "dissents" and "neutrals" of the landowners, lessees and tenants through whose lands it is proposed to construct the line. The agent employs lawyers to draw up a bill for submission to Parliament and to argue the case for the bill before a parliamentary committee (or committees) appointed to consider the proposals.

The bill is very long but the greater part is standard matter

CHESTER AND CREWE JUNCTION RAILWAY,

CAPITAL, £200,000,

IN SHARES OF £50 EACH; DEPOSIT, £1 EACH SHARE.

GEORGE STEPHENSON, ESQ. ENGINEER.

This Railway is intended to form a Junction with the Liverpool and Birmingham Grand Junction Railway at Crewe, t which point it will unite with the Manchester and Cheshire Junction Railway.

The Line has been surveyed under the direction of Mr. Stephenson, who has reported most favourably upon it, both 'om the nature of the ground, which is nearly on a level, and from its not interfering with ornamental property.

The undertaking will provide a communication from Chester, Shropshire, and North Wales, with Manchester and the 1anufacturing Districts, and also with Birmingham, London, and the West of England.

largely applicable to any railway company in any English county. The committee has to be satisfied about a score of aspects of the proposed undertaking—financial, legal, engineering—but especially about the public interest. It must also allow a fair hearing to all parties opposed to the bill. It is necessary, therefore, for the Chairman with some of his fellow directors, the company's solicitor and engineer, together with witnesses, to go to London and stay there throughout the hearings which may take a fortnight or a month.

Opponents may flatly oppose the bill as a whole, or this or that clause in the bill, or seek to insert clauses which will limit the scope of the measure or the powers of the directors. Ill feeling is generated and expenses rise as the fees of the agent and the lawyers are added to the expense of travel to, and residence in, London. The bill may be set back to a later session when the process will begin again. If a bill satisfies the committee or committees, it is introduced in the House of Commons by a private member. Most such bills ultimately are passed by both Houses and become law, though the projects they embody are not necessarily carried into effect.

We pass to particular projects in Cheshire. The Act enabling a company to make a railway states that "the Proprietors shall be one body corporate by the name and style of 'The . . . Railway Company' ", and the progress of railway enterprise in Cheshire may be illustrated by the dates of incorporation of some of the companies:

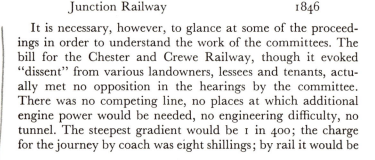

The Grand Junction Railway	1833
The Chester and Birkenhead Railway	1837
The Chester and Crewe Railway	1837
The Manchester and Birmingham Railway	1837
The Chester and Holyhead Railway	1844
The Birkenhead, Lancashire and Cheshire Junction Railway	1846

It is necessary, however, to glance at some of the proceedings in order to understand the work of the committees. The bill for the Chester and Crewe Railway, though it evoked "dissent" from various landowners, lessees and tenants, actually met no opposition in the hearings by the committee. There was no competing line, no places at which additional engine power would be needed, no engineering difficulty, no tunnel. The steepest gradient would be 1 in 400; the charge for the journey by coach was eight shillings; by rail it would be three shillings and sixpence; the time taken by the coach was 2¼ hours; by rail it would be 1 hour.

The Chester and Birkenhead bill on the other hand was opposed before the committee. Hearings took place on eleven days between 12th April and 4th May 1837, and a statement of payments made by the company down to 2nd February 1838 included the following:

	£	s.	d
Law expenses: expenses of witnesses, etc.	3,519	19	9
Parliamentary agents including counsel and parliamentary fees	3,110	0	0
Deputations and travelling expenses	1,037	6	6
Engineering and surveying	3,281	12	10

And some part of the above expense is to be explained by the opposition of the Grand Junction Railway Company which sought to safeguard its interests in south-west Lancashire. If Parliament were to sanction a railway which could drain away the business of Merseyside through Birkenhead, then strong action was needed.

Strong action was indeed taken. A railway from Birkenhead to Birmingham via Chester and Crewe would be shorter than the Grand Junction's line via Warrington. The first application of the Chester and Birkenhead Company was defeated. Though the second was successful, the directors informed their shareholders that only "after a struggle almost unparalleled in the annals of parliamentary warfare in private bills" had the Act incorporating their company been passed.

The Grand Junction Company also saw its interests in south-east Lancashire menaced by proposals to make a railway from Manchester through east Cheshire towards Birmingham which might compete advantageously with their route through Warrington. The situation was complicated for two reasons: first, manufacturing and mineral interests in the Potteries had appealed through John Davenport (M.P. for Stoke-on-Trent in 1832) to the Grand Junction Company to connect their group of towns with the company's line and the company had not yet made an effective response; secondly, two rival companies were seeking to gain the prospective southbound traffic from Manchester through east Cheshire. One of them—variously known as the Birmingham and Manchester, the Manchester and Cheshire Junction or the Manchester and Crewe—proposed to make a line from Manchester via Stockport to join the Grand Junction line at Crewe (which had not

Joseph Locke, 1805–1860, Engineer of the
Grand Junction Railway

yet a station). The other—called at the time the Manchester and South Union or simply South Union—proposed to run its line through Macclesfield towards Burton-on-Trent, but later changed its direction to the Potteries and thence southwards, its ultimate terminal (at that time) being Tamworth on a line still under consideration joining Stafford and Rugby (the Trent Valley).

From December 1835 to July 1836, the directors of the Grand Junction Railway lavished their time, energy, money and influence in support of the Manchester and Crewe Company against the South Union Company. Their bill passed the Commons, and when it became evident that there was a serious risk of its failing in the Lords' committee, the Grand Junction's directors resolved "It is the Company's interest to ensure the passing of the said bill at all hazards even at the cost, if needful, of our engaging not to oppose the South Union Company in the next session". A fortnight later they offered their pledges concerning opposition in the following year "provided such concession ensures the passing of the Crewe Bill *this year*". Their strenuous efforts were however in vain: the Lords' committee rejected the Manchester and Crewe bill.

Similarly the Chester and Birkenhead Company sought to protect its interests by opposing the Grand Junction's bill for taking their line across the Mersey at Fidler's Ferry (1838). The success of such a measure would shorten the Grand Junction line from Liverpool southwards and thus bring it more nearly into competition with the company's line from Birkenhead. As the people of Warrington disliked the project, the Chester and Birkenhead Company decided that it was "their duty to give the utmost effect to the just complaints of the inhabitants of Warrington by supporting them in opposing a measure so likely to prove destructive of the interests of their town". The Grand Junction bill was defeated.

But the Grand Junction Company seized an opportunity when the Chester and Crewe Company revealed the reluctance of its shareholders to subscribe the full capital needed for the completion of their line. Speedy negotiations between the directors of the two lines and a prompt offer of reasonable terms paved the way for a merger. The disheartening situation was explained to a meeting of shareholders at the Royal Hall, Chester in October 1839. The speeches were reported to have been "warm but free from personal asperity". There was no alternative to amalgamation. The shareholders gave their approval. Parliament assented. It was a significant development.

Seen from Birkenhead and Chester, railway enterprise might seek a southward junction, say, at Madeley. Seen from Manchester southbound traffic might flow towards the Potteries, Stone, Stafford or Tamworth. But the Grand Junction was bringing the Chester traffic (and potentially the Holyhead traffic) into its own system to make a junction at a place soon to be called Crewe. Only a year later, authority was gained to bring the Manchester traffic in at the same place. The Grand Junction combined with the London and Birmingham Company to form the London and North Western Railway Company in 1846. In 1848 the North Staffordshire Railway Company linked Stoke-on-Trent with Crewe and in 1858 a line was opened between Shrewsbury and Crewe. As already stated, railway development in Cheshire had its own logic. The Grand Junction line was like a great river to which other lines were destined to be tributaries.

Unification of short railways was, of course, proceeding elsewhere (and notably in Lancashire) and there were still further proposals for the construction of new lines. For several years the L.N.W.R. sought to dominate all railway development in the region it had marked out for its own. By opposing here, providing capital there, diverting traffic in one place and insisting on the routing of traffic to its own advantage in another, it became feared and hated by the shareholders of the smaller companies.

At times it was challenged by the Great Western Railway Company which had contrived to bind together the smaller enterprises between Hereford and Chester in an effort to gain a way to the north. The Great Western in fact not only reached Chester, but extended its sway to Birkenhead, by taking over the Chester and Birkenhead Railway Company. This company had never known the prosperity of other railway enterprises. It had no access to Manchester and the industrial towns of Lancashire till the opening of the Birkenhead, Lancashire and Cheshire Junction Railway, no opportunity for development of the coal traffic from North Wales till the Shrewsbury and the Mold lines into Chester were completed; and the Grand Junction Company had boycotted it. The Birkenhead Advertiser in March 1860 spoke of two powerful wooers and the embarrassed comment "how happy could I be with either were t'other dear charmer away", but it gave its support to the Great Western.

Much more might be written of the relations between the North Staffordshire Railway Company and the Grand Junction and the London and North Western, of that Company's link-up with the North Western at Crewe and at Chebsey (Norton Bridge), of its difficult route through east Cheshire to Macclesfield and thence to Manchester, and of the creation of lines for suburban services to Manchester. It is sufficient for our purpose to note that railway construction in Cheshire—as elsewhere—excited struggles and bitterness between rival Boards of Directors (and their shareholders), that the most powerful and most purposeful company was the Grand Junction (and after 1846 the London and North Western) and that by 1850, from the point of view of railways the most important place in Cheshire was Crewe.

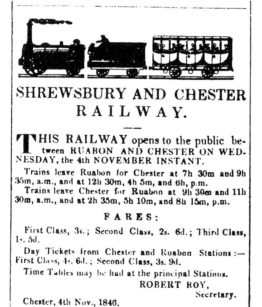

SHREWSBURY AND CHESTER RAILWAY.

THIS RAILWAY opens to the public between RUABON AND CHESTER ON WEDNESDAY, the 4th NOVEMBER INSTANT.

Trains leave Ruabon for Chester at 7h 30m and 9h 35m, a.m., and at 12h 30m, 4h 5m, and 6h, p.m.

Trains leave Chester for Ruabon at 9h 30m and 11h 30m, a.m., and at 2h 35m, 5h 10m, and 8h 15m, p.m.

FARES:

First Class, 3s.; Second Class, 2s. 6d.; Third Class, 1s. 5d.

Day Tickets from Chester and Ruabon Stations:— First Class, 4s. 6d.; Second Class, 3s. 9d.

Time Tables may be had at the principal Stations.

ROBERT ROY,
Secretary.

Chester, 4th Nov., 1846.

Shrewsbury and Chester Railway

Chapter Two
RAILWAY CONSTRUCTION

The Act of Parliament enabling a company to make a railway gave it "power to enter, to survey and take lands, and to make a railway . . . to construct, make, set up in, upon, across, under or over . . . streets . . . roads, rivers, canals . . . inclined planes, tunnels, embankments, bridges, arches, piers, aqueducts, viaducts . . . and to divert rivers and canals".

Once the Act had received the royal assent, the directors turned their attention to the services of the civil engineer, the mechanical engineer and the builder of coaches. Civil engineering was a relatively new profession. Military engineers had made roads, earthworks and tunnels for centuries, but the construction of canals posed problems remote from the military art such as embankments, deep cuttings and aqueducts. The solution of these problems produced a body of knowledge which was of great value to the early railway engineers, and the construction of the Liverpool and Manchester Railway itself, as a contemporary wrote, "added no small stock of operative experience to the science of the age". Civil engineering was beginning to creep into university studies, but the two Stephensons, Locke and other railway builders of the period had no academic training.

Now a railway differed from a canal in that it had of course to mount inclines, but as smooth steel wheels running on smooth steel rails produced little friction, it became necessary to relate the power and weight of the locomotive to the weight of the train it had to haul and to the steepness of the incline it had to mount, that is to say to study locomotive performance on gradients. This led to considerations of speed and of fuel consumption on the one hand, and to the avoidance of steep gradients by going round obstacles or by deep cuttings or by tunneling on the other. Gradients came to dominate the mind of the engineer as he planned the line of the railway. In some counties, it was constantly necessary to balance cost of construction against cost of operation.

Though the surface of Cheshire presented few serious problems in railway construction, gradients necessarily influenced all the undertakings. The steepest on the Grand Junction line was that between Madeley summit and Crewe viz. 1 in 177; on the Chester and Crewe line it was 1 in 400; on the Chester and Birkenhead 1 in 330; on the Hooton to Helsby link 1 in

151; between Crewe and Stockport 1 in 284; and it was argued
against the line passing through Macclesfield that it involved
a gradient of 1 in 101. When alternative routes between
Chester and Birkenhead were under consideration, George
Stephenson plotted profiles of the two proposed lines on a
single sheet and showed that although his proposal was the
longer, it involved less climbing. His line was accepted.

Further, all bridges must be related to gradients: the Grand
Junction line had to be kept low enough to pass *under* the
Bridgewater canal near Preston Brook; the Chester and Crewe
line had to pass *under* the Shropshire Union canal near Chester;
and whenever the line passed *over* a river (as at Dutton, Holmes
Chapel and Congleton), the height of the viaduct or bridge
was obviously governed by the engineer's decision as to the
height at which the track should be maintained. Most of these
problems had been foreseen when the hearing of an application before a parliamentary committee began.

The problems surrounding the acquisition of a long strip
of land had also been understood: applicants had to state the
exact length of the desired strips concerning which landowners, lessees or tenants "dissented". Their opposition could
not be maintained, but adequate compensation both monetary
and in easements (e.g. the provision of bridges where a line
divided one part of an estate from another), had to be made.

The work of construction tends to fall into a pattern. The
engineer "stakes out" the line, divides it into sections and
draws up a specification for each section; tenders are invited;
contractors are chosen; agreements between the directors and
the contractors are signed. Broadly, the directors provide the
land, the rails and the chairs for the permanent way; the
contractors provide everything else.

The contractors assemble their men, material, tools, equipment and horses in their several sections and start operations.
For the whole line or for part of the line the directors appoint a
resident engineer who watches the progress of the work, insists
on detailed execution of the agreements, reports periodically
to the directors, certifies the amount of work done, and
authorises proportionate payments to the contractors. When
the work is completed, the contractors have to maintain the
lines in their respective sections during the first year of use.
Only then do they receive their final payments.

Provided that the land is available when the agreement is
signed, and that the contractor has a large enough labour
force, expectations may be promptly and smoothly fulfilled.

Commonly, however, some sort of "trouble", trifling or serious, occurs. Typical hindrances arise from the failure of investors to subscribe the full sums they have promised, from unforeseen difficulties in civil engineering, from dilatoriness on the part of the contractor, and, of course, from the weather which may not only hinder the work of the navvies, but also flood part of the track in the cuttings and render operations impossible. All these hindrances occurred at one point or another in the construction of the Cheshire railways and, if bad weather is too commonly cited as an excuse for delay, it must be allowed that the autumn and winter rains of 1839 were serious enough to affect the progress of work both in the Wirral and between Chester and Crewe. Finally, the navvies were not a perfectly disciplined body: they had occasional "randies" during which most of them did no work at all.

The sections of the Grand Junction in Cheshire beginning in the south, were referred to as the Basford contract, the Wharton contract, the Hartford contract, the Preston Brook contract and the Warrington contract. The construction of the great viaduct over the Weaver at Dutton was regarded as a separate undertaking for which a separate contract was needed. In illustration of the nature of railway construction in the county we treat a few of these contracts in some detail.

The agreement for the Hartford contract was made on 25th June 1834, when Benjamin Seeds (father and son) of Prescot, Lancashire, signed an undertaking to complete seven miles, three furlongs of railway by 1st April 1837 for the sum of £92,066 (and to forfeit £30 a day for each day they might be in arrears). The capital sum was to be paid over to the contractors in instalments every two months according to the proportion of material used and work done, less 10 per cent, and the contractors were to maintain everything in perfect order for twelve months after the engineer's certificate of completion had been signed.

The Grand Junction Company was to provide the land, the rails and the chairs, and to forward rails and chairs by canal to certain points as required.

The Seeds were to provide all other material and equipment necessary for the work. They would observe the stipulations of various Acts of Parliament, especially those concerning the River Weaver; they would not injure the river, the canal or the towing path; they would do no harm to the turnpike roads which had to be crossed; they would accept responsibility for

Grand Junction Railway. The Dutton Viaduct over the valley of the Weaver. Coloured engraving by Radclyffe after T. Creswick

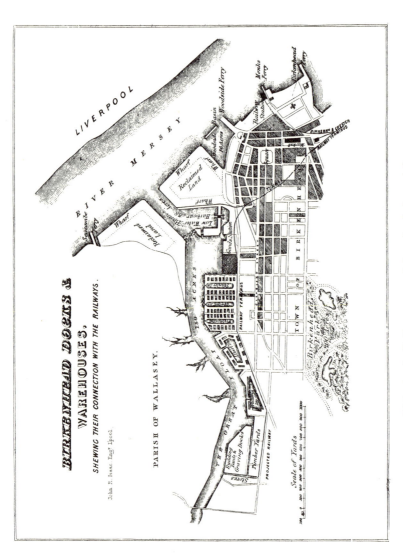

Birkenhead. Railways extended to the docks and ferry

all accidents and submit to the engineer's ruling in all disputes.

A plan was provided; the exact starting point in Acton and the finishing point in Wharton were defined by reference to the roads to be crossed. The gradients (starting in Acton) were stated thus:

$$
\begin{array}{rll}
2,530 \text{ yards} & \text{rising} & 1 \text{ in } 330 \\
1,430 \text{ ,,} & \text{——— level} \\
1,760 \text{ ,,} & \text{rising} & 1 \text{ in } 440 \\
1,364 \text{ ,,} & \text{,,} & 1 \text{ in } 1,585 \\
1,760 \text{ ,,} & \text{falling} & 1 \text{ in } 330 \\
550 \text{ ,,} & \text{——— level} \\
3,588 \text{ ,,} & \text{rising} & 1 \text{ in } 600 \\
\hline
12,982 \text{ ,,} & \text{or } 7\frac{3}{8} \text{ miles}
\end{array}
$$

The track was described as 12,000 yards in cuttings and 982 on embankments, and the following estimates were given "for information", the directors not being responsible for their accuracy:

80,000 cubic yards of ballast
48,000 stone blocks
1,964 wooden sleepers
48,000 pieces of patent felt
103,856 iron spikes
96,000 oak pins

Ten drawings of bridges were provided—one for a five-arch bridge of Runcorn stone over the Weaver, the others over or under the railway at various places, all those over the line being at least 15 feet 6 inches in height. There were also to be a number of cast-iron bridges for carrying footroads over the track.

In the agreement a good deal of detail was incorporated concerning the bridges, ballast, slopes of embankments, the disposal of soil from cuttings, the planting of hedges, the provision of drainage, the provision of mile posts and quarter mile posts and the building of three cottages. Finally there was a restrictive clause concerning the method (but not the rate) of payment to the workers in the contractors' employ.

A similar agreement concerning part of the Preston Brook contract throws more light on the materials used: gates at foot crossings must be made of Heart of Oak or best Memel timber; mortar must be made of best Welsh lime mixed with clean, sharp sand in the proportion of 1 to 2; for the double track there will be two sleepers or four blocks for every linear yard; for 2,500 yards of embankment, therefore, there will be 5,000 sleepers each 9 feet by 10 inches by 4½ inches; and for 5,814 yards of cutting or solid ground 23,256 blocks will be needed and 46,512 oak pins. The pins will be of oak and made to fit exactly the holes drilled in the blocks. Two wrought iron bolts with mushroom heads are required for each chair.

The most difficult operation (in the Cheshire part of the line) was the construction of the Dutton viaduct over the river Weaver (between the stations of Acton Bridge and Preston Brook) by David McIntosh of Bloomsbury Square, London, the original contract being in the sum of £54,440. The viaduct was not as long as those at Stockport and Holmes Chapel, nor was it as high as that at Stockport, but it involved legal restrictions and technical problems. The rights of the Weaver Navigation had, of course, to be scrupulously respected and as one difficulty after another arose, the Weaver Trustees had to be consulted and conciliated. The strata below the valley bottom lacked the solidity necessary to support the weight of the bridge; the suitability of Locke's design was questioned and other engineers were called in for consultation.

When detailed inspection on the site was decided on, floods thwarted the inspectors and, on a second occasion the waters washed away the river bank at a vital point. A debate ensued as to whether the piers should rest on piles or whether it was necessary to get down through the marl to a more solid foundation. A decision in favour of piers was embodied in an agreement signed in February 1834, but as George Stephenson was still not satisfied about the safety of the project, work was suspended during the summer and autumn of that year. After still further alterations made at the instance of the Weaver Navigation engineer, the work approached completion.

A second problem—it was in the Preston Brook contract—was unusual rather than technically difficult: below the village of Preston on the Hill, the railway engineers had decided to run their line along a slight depression in which already lay the Bridgewater canal and the Kekwick Brook. At Preston Brook that canal makes a V-turn and has warehouses and wharves for its junction with the Trent and Mersey canal. Just at this V-turn the railway line had to be thrust *under* the Bridgewater canal and at the same time avoid flooding from the brook.

Aqueducts were not uncommon—there were at least three within fifty miles of Preston Brook—but they had been constructed as aqueducts at heights determined by the engineers. The solution adopted revealed some interesting features. In the first place, the level of the railway line (as already stated) had to be kept low enough for it to pass under the canal. Next, the railway directors hoped to have the work done during the period when the canal water was drawn off for annual repairs "which will shortly take place". Many months elapsed before the work was even begun and indeed a temporary canal had to be built to avoid a stoppage of the canal traffic. The directors instructed the contractor to build the aqueduct askew at about 59° between the directions of the canal and the railway. The towing path was to pass over the railway by means of stone arches; the water was to be in a cast-iron trough formed of ribs and plates; the trough was to be made "watertight with gasken well saturated in the best tar and with fine borings, sulphur and sal ammoniac mixed to a proper consistency". The trough and exterior iron work were to have three coats of good mineral paint.

Relations between the trustees of the Bridgewater canal and the directors of the Grand Junction Railway were—as might be expected—often strained. There were disagreements, halts in the railway's work, instructions to the contractor to go ahead with his work "as no answer can be got from the trustees", and even stronger instructions when for the second time the trustees served him with a notice not to proceed.

A third problem was primarily one for negotiation between directors of railway companies. By the spring of 1834, plans were completed for the line as far northwards as the parish of Moore. That the Grand Junction would continue to Warrington and proceed thence to join the Liverpool and Manchester railway had been understood from the beginning. It remained to determine a site for a bridge across the Mersey and to plot the approach from Moore down to the bridge. But the site (and therefore the approach) would be governed by the link which was to connect the two railways, for Warrington lay some four or five miles south of the Liverpool and Manchester line and the link had apparently not been settled in detail when the grand project was conceived.

Now a potential link existed, for there was already a Warrington and Newton Railway Company; its route was suitable; it was in fact actually in operation. Whether the Grand Junction should, or could, run its trains over the lines of this company, or try to acquire the company, or build a new line of its own exercised the minds of the directors for many months. The Warrington and Newton Railway Company was in a strong bargaining position. The Grand Junction was not without resources. In May 1834, Stephenson was instructed to consider a route that should avoid the Warrington and Newton line; in July, Locke was directed to "survey the country between the Mersey and the Liverpool and Manchester Railway and report as to the possibility of choosing a communication independently of the Warrington and Newton line". A crossing of the Mersey at Fidler's Ferry was considered; the assent of the landowners and occupiers on the Cheshire side to the construction of a line to the Ferry was obtained, and David McIntosh, builder of the Dutton viaduct, submitted a tender (£29,000) for the building of a bridge at the Ferry.

By this time, the directors of the Warrington and Newton Railway were willing to confer about the disposal of their railway. The Grand Junction Company acquired it and decided to make the connection between the two lines at Bank Quay station in Warrington. The last length of the Grand Junction line in Cheshire—down to the site of the bridge—was now planned in detail and William Mackenzie's tender in the sum of £43,000 was accepted in April 1835.

We return to the Wirral where George Stephenson's plan for a line between Birkenhead and Chester had been adopted and divided into four sections and contracts allocated:
  Bebington contract: Messrs. Bowers, Murray & Brownbill.
  Bromborough and Eastham contract: the same.
  Sutton contract: Messrs. Henry and Clements.
  Moston and Chester contract: contractor's name
    suppressed.
By October 1838, the directors reported favourably on the work of Bowers, Murray and Brownbill especially in respect of the crossing of Bromborough Pool. "The mass of masonry," they said, "the formidable height of the embankment and the peculiar character of the Vale into which the tidal waters flow with the doubt which might reasonably be entertained of the quality of the substratum, demanded great attention, energy and dispatch in the construction of the work". Yet "all difficulty had been overcome".

The following table affords some idea of the labour force employed in the Wirral:

The Warrington Viaduct

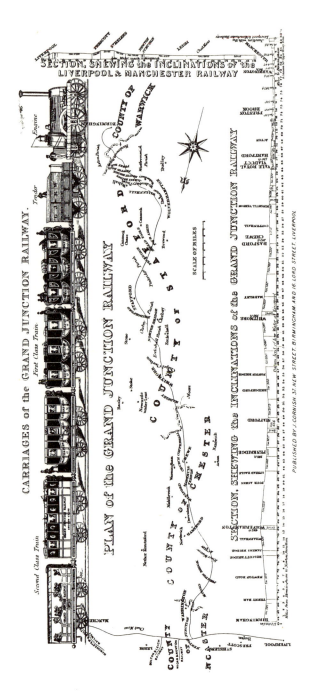

Plan of the Grand Junction Railway Company 1837

Contract			April 1839		October 1839	
			Men	Horses	Men	Horses
	miles	*chains*				
Bebington	2	32	300	17	312	17
Bromborough	3	37	220	41	418	43
Sutton	3	17	150	18	c400	50
Moston & Chester	5	37	447	32	900	40
			1,117	128	2,030	150

Another form of contract was used by the Manchester and South Junction Railway Company for John Brogden (of Sussex Gardens, Hyde Park, Middlesex) who on 6th November 1845 signed an agreement for the construction of the Altrincham Branch from Castle Field, Manchester to Hale Moss. It mentioned no inclusive sum for the $7\frac{3}{4}$ mile length of line, but provided an exceedingly detailed statement of work to be done, together with twenty-four drawings, and the prices at which no less than a hundred items were to be carried out. There were 153,489 cubic yards to be excavated and 126,321 cubic yards of embankment. The operation was to be completed by 1st June 1847. Payment to the contractor was to be made in the first instance after eight weeks and then at intervals of four weeks. The only reference to the workmen is a statement that should the contractor default, the company might take over and employ them. (That is there was no reference to their rates, places or methods of payment.)

Three tunnels must be mentioned. The first was no more than a short extension of the Chester and Birkenhead Railway Company's line. In October 1838, the directors informed the shareholders that their company must "get the Mersey crossing under complete control and that at the best point". The Woodside ferry, they stated, ought to be acquired. From that date onward they sought to purchase both the Woodside Ferry and the Monk's Ferry. Since, however, their terminal was not at the water's edge, it would be a great advantage if passengers could be taken direct from Grange Lane station to the ferry. In order to achieve that end, it was necessary to make a tunnel under the town. George Stephenson's advice was sought: after some delay the line was extended to the Monk's Ferry and opened in October 1844.

The second tunnel, the Woodhead, was a vastly greater undertaking. At the extreme eastern point of the county, the Manchester and Sheffield Company's railway passed up the valley of a little stream, the Etherow, burrowed under the Pennines at Woodhead in Cheshire and emerged near Dunford Bridge in Yorkshire. Measuring more than three miles in length, it was at the time the longest in England. Because of the strata through which it was bored, it was the most difficult to make. Though five shafts were sunk so that the men could labour at twelve points at once, the work took six years (1839–45) to complete. A second line parallel with the first was made in 1847–52.

A third tunnel had to be made in order to lay the Chester–Warrington line under the high ground between Frodsham and Norton. It is known as Halton (or Sutton) tunnel, was constructed in 1848 and is about a mile and a furlong in length. It was the scene of a serious accident in 1851.

There were two other tunnels, namely one of 300 yards length just south of Edgeley station, Stockport, and a short one under the Shropshire Union Canal between Chester and Waverton on the Crewe line.

It was no small achievement in the 1830s and 1840s to have bored through the hills, to have made high embankments and deep cuttings, but the construction of lofty viaducts revealed man's victory over natural obstacles, "an extraordinary triumph of Art over the difficulties of Nature" as Mr. Ormsby Gore said in opening the Dee viaduct near Ruabon, on the Shrewsbury line. Accordingly the laying of the last stone of a great bridge was usually carried out ceremonially.

In view of the size of the Dutton viaduct (1,400 feet in length, 20 arches each of 63 feet span), the difficulties overcome and the absence of accidents among the workers, the last step was deemed worthy of a public occasion. On Friday 2nd December 1836, amid a great crowd of people, Mr. Heyworth, the senior director present, accepted the trowel, performed the operation, praised Locke and stated that "in the erection of the greatest and first structure of its kind in the kingdom, no life or limb had been sacrificed". In the evening, according to the Chester Courant, "the viaduct was illuminated with torches and fireworks were displayed in great abundance during which time the workmen were regaled with a good dinner and excellent cheer".

Similarly the completion of the Stockport viaduct was an occasion for celebration. At noon on Monday 21st December 1842, a great company headed by Mr. Ashton, Chairman of the

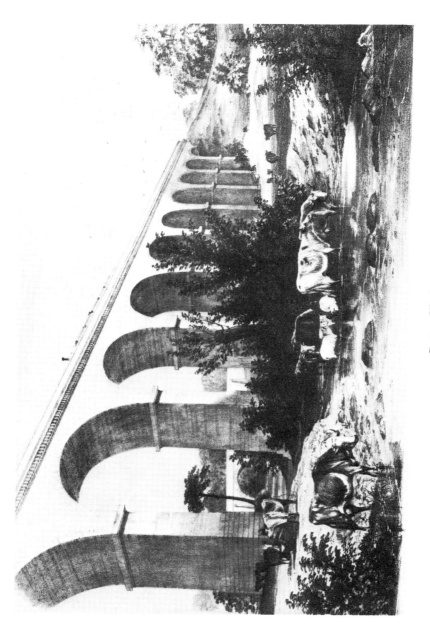

Dutton Viaduct

Stockport Viaduct

Directors of the Manchester and Birmingham Railway Company, and the two M.P.s for the borough, walked in procession across the beflagged viaduct to the south end. Mr. Holmes, one of the contractors (Tomkinson and Holmes) handed Mr. Ashton a silver trowel; the mortar was spread and the stone was lowered into its place "amidst the volleys of cannon and the cheering and shouting of all in attendance". A select company had a splendid banquet in a pavilion erected on the line, and "forty-five workmen were liberally regaled with the old English fare of good roast beef, plum pudding and strong ale the next day at the George Inn, Heaton Norris".

We give a summary of the building of the remaining lines. The railway from Manchester to Crewe was opened as far as Stockport in 1840 and as far as Crewe in 1841. Among the obstacles to be surmounted were the series of tributaries of the Mersey viz the Ladybrook, the Dean, the Bollin, the Peover, the Dane and the Wheelock. Each of these required a viaduct, that over the Dane at Holmes Chapel being the greatest (1794 feet in length, 23 arches each of 63 feet span). The parallel line constructed by the North Stafford Railway Company joining Macclesfield with the Potteries (1849) also had two lofty viaducts: at North Rode crossing the Dane valley by a series of 20 arches 110 feet above the bed of the river, and at Congleton the Daneshaw viaduct of 10 arches of about the same height.

The modern use of mechanical transport, mechanical excavators and other equipment has made the undertakings of the 1830s and 1840s appear diminutive. In their day, they were very considerable achievements. Avoiding the ancient highways, they made smooth new communications from the bank of the Mersey at Birkenhead, Warrington and Stockport to the south of the county, a new way skirting the Pennine slopes through Macclesfield towards the Potteries, and a network of lines in north-east Cheshire.

Though the county is relatively level, there are few stretches of any length where the surface did not need some adjustment to ensure a smooth track. Even the short line from Chester to Birkenhead called for the excavation of 634,340 cubic yards of earth and rock for one route or 800,990 for the other (as the directors might choose), and their removal to embankments, while in the shorter length of the Preston Brook contract, the directors' estimate of the volume of earth to be removed was 355,718 cubic yards. On the few miles of the Hartford contract 80,000 cubic yards of ballast had to be laid, and in the track 48,000 stone blocks (to hold the chairs) had to be inserted. Thousands of tons of stone had to be loaded into carts or lorries at the quarries and unloaded at the sites of the bridges. For the Stockport viaduct, 400,000 cubic feet of stone were said to have been used and 11,000,000 bricks. Rails for the Grand Junction track weighed 50 pounds to the yard, for the Manchester and South Junction 65 pounds to the yard.

Gunpowder was, of course, used to blast rock, but the energy required for the pick-and-shovel work of excavation, for 'pitching' the spoil into wagons, and for handling the masonry, the rails, the sleepers and the stone blocks was supplied by gangs of workers who were recruited, directed and paid by the contractors. There were masons, bricklayers, carpenters (for the great frames on which the arches were built) and a much larger number of men known as 'navvies' whose dress, habits and outlook made them a distinct social class. Some of them were drawn from the localities through which the lines passed; more came from a distance; not a few were Irish or Scots; but Englishmen also moved freely from one contract to another.

With these men the railway companies had no direct contact, but directly or indirectly, company policy might affect the men. Steady progress was demanded by the directors and as one contractor after another was pressed to show 'greater expedition' or 'greater diligence' in the execution of his agreement, the directors were insisting on greater or more efficient use of man power. Further—and this is creditable to the Grand Junction Company—though the directors made no reference to the men's rates of pay, they insisted that "wages shall be paid in money, not in tickets on any Tommy shop, Beer Shop or Public House, nor shall wages be paid in any such place". The Manchester and Sheffield Company allowed the evil practice of Tommy shops at Woodhead. In view, however, of the isolated position of the undertaking, it may have been impossible to avoid.

Moreover, though the contractors were liable for all accidents, the Grand Junction sub-engineers were informed in 1836 that "in case of any accident happening to workmen employed on the line, the Company will pay all expenses consequent on their relief from the nearest infirmary or dispensary". In November of that year, the company paid over £44 for "surgical attendance" to labourers hurt on the line near Warrington, and in March 1837, £10 was paid to

GREAT WESTERN RAILWAY.
CHESTER CUP DAY.

A FAST SPECIAL TRAIN will leave the General Station, Chester, on WEDNESDAY, the 6th May, at 6 p.m., for Birmingham, Leamington, Oxford, and London, arriving at Birmingham at 8. 25, Oxford 9. 55, and London at 11. 30.

Ordinary Tickets will be available for this Train.

Apply for Tickets at the Great Western Booking Office Window at the General Station.

Chester Courant 6th May 1857, Chester Cup

VIA GREAT WESTERN RAILWAY.
THE GREAT TREAT OF THE SEASON
TO THE
CRYSTAL PALACE, SYDENHAM,
FOR 11s. 6D.
ON MONDAY, SEPTEMBER 20TH.

A SPECIAL EXPRESS TRAIN will leave Chester at 9.20 a.m.; Wrexham, 9.45 a.m.; Llangollen Road, 10.5 a.m.; and Oswestry at 9.45 a.m., (Oswestry passengers join the Special Train at Gobowen) for

LONDON.
FARES FOR THE DOUBLE JOURNEY.

Closed Carriages, 11s.   First Class, 18s. 6d.

Returning from Paddington Station at 7 a.m. on Saturday, the 25th instant.

Tickets will be issued with the above for the Crystal Palace, Sydenham, First Class, 1s. 6d.; Second Class, 1s.; Third Class, 6d., including Railway Fare and Admission to the Palace.

Early application for Tickets is requested at the Great Western Railway Offices, Eastgate-street, Chester; at the Stations; and from JOHN ERVING, 41, Norton-street, Liverpool.

At the same time to Shrewsbury, Wolverhampton, Birmingham, Leamington, Oxford, and Reading. See bills.

Chester Courant 15th Sept. 1858
Cheap Fare to Crystal Palace

the widow of a labourer who had been killed while working in the Preston Brook contract. Again, while the housing of gangs of workers was usually forced on the contractors—they made shanties and huts—the company considered the "expediency of assisting" contractors to make "temporary dwellings" for the men. The Chester and Holyhead Railway Company also showed some regard for the welfare of the men engaged in making their line: contractors were directed to erect huts where local village accommodation was insufficient and to pay wages on fixed dates and wholly in money. It must, however, be allowed that the Grand Junction and Holyhead Companies set a higher standard than several other companies.

For the most part, the conditions under which the men worked were degrading. They had neither the settled comforts of home, nor the discipline of army units, nor the weekly wages of the agricultural labourer and the urban craftsman, nor in many cases the parochial ministrations of the churches. At the Woodhead tunnel, the general state of affairs among the men —their accidents, their illnesses, the gross abuses of the local Tommy shops, the drunken affrays—became notorious. In the country as a whole, the navvies were regarded as quarrelsome, unruly, hard-drinking fellows whose occasional outbursts had to be quelled by the military.

In 1839, a very serious disturbance broke out in Wirral. The origin, according to a newspaper report, lay in the disappearance of a man carrying wages for the navvies employed by one of the contractors for the Chester and Birkenhead Railway. A successor appointed to bring money to the men, was subjected to demands for the wages they had lost. These he would not, or could not, pay. He was struck; violence spread; Irishmen attacked Englishmen; non-strikers were mutilated. A large gang "possessed themselves of the entire village of Sutton" and pillaged the inn where a harvest supper was being prepared. More than two hundred soldiers were brought from Liverpool and Chester to restore order and twenty-seven of the ringleaders were lodged in Birkenhead gaol. There is some editorial reserve as to whether Irishmen or Englishmen were the more responsible for the violence, and the report ends by attributing the outbreak to the "invariable turbulence of temper" the navvies display "as the termination of their labour approaches".

Judged by modern standards, most of the companies and contractors appear to have been gravely indifferent to the welfare of the masses of men who did the hard manual work of constructing the railways. That view though largely true needs qualification, for the same judgement may be passed on other employers of the 1830s and 1840s. England was slowly advancing towards regulation of the conditions of employment, but the first section of the population to be protected was the children who worked in the cotton mills (at Stockport, for example). Adult males came last. There were enlightened employers who found a measure of social welfare not incompatible with the making of profits, but conditions in the mines and in many of the factories were as bad as those in the railway cuttings and the tunnels, though miners and factory hands usually received weekly wages.

Moreover, it would be an over-simplification to assert that the companies merely defined the ends while the contractors supplied the means, for the role of the engineer must not be overlooked. It was in the light of his judgement and advice that the directors acted. By the terms of the agreements, his decision on all aspects of civil engineering was final. It was he who reported progress or delay in the execution of contracts. It was his estimate of work which determined the amounts of the payments periodically paid over to the contractors. And when contractors advanced the justice of allowing payments towards the cost of material bought expressly for, say, a bridge and already waiting at the site, but not yet embodied in the structure, it lay with the engineer to determine whether their case should be presented favourably to the directors.

So far as can be gathered from the minutes of the directors' meetings, Locke acted honourably. The Seeds' agreement for the Hartford contract stated that payment should be made every two months . . . "for material *used*". An appeal by that firm (in respect of material on the site) was refused in January 1835, but in December of that year, they were granted an advance of £700 and in April 1836, not only the Seeds but also John Stephenson, contractor for the Basford section and Thomas Brassey and Co., contractors operating further south, were granted allowances "to such an extent and with such precautions as Mr. Locke shall find sufficient to protect the company from risk".

An attempt to apportion responsibility for deplorable circumstances must take full account of the contractor's position. He had to work against a time limit for exceeding which he would forfeit £30 or £50 a day. He was subject to the risks of labour shortage—navvies were in great demand in Lancashire—and labour "troubles": randies and quarrels—and, of course, bad weather. Even when his work was completed, he had to maintain every sleeper, chair, fence and drain in good condition for a whole year before he received final payment. He needed, therefore, large capital resources. Still more capital was required when payment for materials "on site" was made tardily and reluctantly. And when payment for work done was received at intervals of a month—in Seeds' case two months—it is not surprising if he paid wages at similar intervals, with the result that men contracted big debts for food and, on receipt of wages, turned to bouts of heavy drinking. For truck and Tommy shops no defence can be offered; indifference to the physical and moral welfare of employees was typical of employers of the period; in so far as the gross evils associated with the navvies are attributable to the system of wage-paying, the companies must share blame equally with the contractors.

Since the purpose of the railway was transport, the attention of the directors was concentrated (in the early days) primarily on the making of a track along which locomotives might haul trains. Stations were necessary halting places; terminal stations needed sheds for carriages, for engines and soon for goods; fares had, of course, to be paid and, in the earliest days of the Grand Junction line, the "conductor" collected them, but it became necessary to have booking offices. As for the comfort and convenience of travellers awaiting the arrival of trains at stations, the early records make no mention of either platforms or shelter.

In December 1837, the directors of the Grand Junction company recommended "measures for providing improved accommodation" at stations for passengers. In October 1840, the engineer of the Chester and Birkenhead company admitted regretfully that while progress had been made with the station at Birkenhead, the station buildings at Chester were in "a more backward state": there was a temporary wooden hut for a booking office but no "passenger shed". Six months later, he confessed that a wooden hut had been used for five months, but he was able to add that "latterly some houses (in Brook Street) have been converted into an office and waiting room, and considerable accommodation provided for the comfort and convenience of passengers by the erection of a large shed and landing stage" (platform).

But the situation called for more than a "large shed", for at Chester four distinct railway companies had decided to establish termini. That all four companies ran their trains to one point was a step towards good sense; that all four should expect terminal facilities—engine sheds, coach sheds, booking offices, station staff—was natural. Three problems therefore faced the companies, namely:

1. the conversion of the station at Chester into a real junction instead of a mere meeting place;

2. the provision of shelter and some minimum of convenience and amenity in the station;

3. co-operative or even unitary management of the station.

The first two might be attained in one grand operation. The third involved rivalries and ambitions: it might take time to reach a solution suitable to all parties.

In 1840, the Grand Junction company which had already arranged with the London and Birmingham company for a joint station in Birmingham, proposed the erection of a joint station in place of the "temporary station" at Chester. The Chester and Birkenhead company agreed in principle but rejected the actual plan proposed and decided to go ahead with plans of its own, using (as mentioned above) some houses in Brook Street.

In December 1846, a Joint Committee consisting of representatives of the four companies was formed and within a few months approved plans for the erection of a joint station, a group of goods sheds and a bridge over the rails at the end of Brook Street. Thomas Brassey's tender for building the station was accepted. He failed to get the contract for the bridge but later obtained that for the goods station.

The new station was begun in August 1847 and opened exactly a year later. Both externally and internally it was regarded as "a noble pile of buildings". The facade—said at the time to be the longest in England—was 1,050 feet in length, and there were wings "formed by projecting arcades with iron roofs, appropriated to private and public vehicles awaiting the arrival of trains". The number of offices and rooms exceeded fifty. There was a cloak-room—one of the first in England; there were w.c.s; there was a refreshment room managed by a Mr. Hobday who paid the station committee £500 a year for the right. Indeed, the station was "adapted for the purpose of developing all those facilities and conveniences which are the characteristics of the railway system".

On the more technical side, the compound terminus was converted into a "through station" by laying two main lines for common use right through the station. And a platform 750 feet in length was made chiefly "for departing trains", with a second platform measuring some 450 feet. Both were covered by iron roofs.

The Joint Committee did not achieve unitary management of the station without bitterness. The companies differed over the proportion of representatives they should have, and later there was resentment over the policy of the London and North Western company, for its wealth and size gave it predominant influence. The committee, however, achieved a notable step in a decision that the station master should be a "neutral", that is to say, he should not be recruited from any of the participant companies. Even that prudent measure did not prevent quarrels inside the station over competing interests: Wolverhampton, for example, could be reached via Shrewsbury or via Crewe. Rival companies instructed their booking clerks about prices of tickets for the journeys and placards to be exhibited in the station. There were disgraceful scenes in 1849 when the clerk of the Shrewsbury railway was dragged out of his office and his tickets thrown after him.

Circumstances at Crewe were wholly different from those at Chester, for in 1840 Crewe can scarcely be said to have existed. Engineers preparing a route linking Chester with the Grand Junction Railway had decided to meet that line at a point where it crossed the boundary between the parishes of Church Coppenhall and Monks' Coppenhall. A mile or two away stood a tiny hamlet called Crewe and an ancient mansion, Crewe Hall. To the station (built a quarter of a mile south of the meeting point) the name Crewe was given. Shortly afterwards the Manchester and Birmingham line came into the Grand Junction system at the same point as the Chester line.

In relation to railway development, this was the beginning of the greatest centre of communications in the west of England. In relation to the history of Cheshire, the significance of the junction dates from the decision of the Grand Junction Company to remove its locomotive works from Liverpool to Crewe.

Nantwich, Middlewich and Northwich had been centres of the salt industry as far back as Domesday and were still market towns. The Potteries had developed a great industry in earthenware and had valuable deposits of coal. Crewe had no antiquity, no industry, no coalpits, no canal wharves. It was planned and built for the sole purpose of housing the employees engaged in the railway's locomotive workshops and

Chester & Birkenhead Railway Interior of General Railway Station, Chester

Lithograph by Tait, Crewe Station, L. & N.W. Railway

their families. Experience had shown that locomotives needed frequent repairs and that repairs could be effected and new engines built more cheaply by the railway companies than by outside contractors. The company's locomotive sheds and repair shops at Edge Hill (Liverpool) were inconveniently sited. Crewe would be a better place: it was nearer the centre of traffic and afforded room for indefinite expansion. In the acute angle between the lines leading to Warrington and to Chester, the railway works were built; in the fields west and north of the station, a town was laid out; and to that town in March 1843, the workers and their families were brought at the company's expense.

Between 1837 and 1843, therefore, the stopping place called Crewe was no more than a wayside station. The growth of the town and still more the increasing importance of the railway junction made necessary some extensive changes in the station. The exterior on the Nantwich Road was unimpressive; the interior had never been a mere *group* of terminals: for the Grand Junction and for the Chester and Crewe companies it had been from the start a "through" station, and after 1846, the London and North Western Railway Company dominated the system which connected not only Liverpool, Manchester and Birmingham with one another and also with London, but soon Glasgow with the capital also.

In 1845–46 there were extensive changes and "better accommodation for ladies". The proprietor of the Crewe Arms, which stood just outside the station, was allowed a room in the station for the sale of refreshments, and in 1858 refreshment rooms were provided. In the 1850s the station was described as "noble and handsome . . . about half a mile east from the town". It had "offices, waiting rooms and every accommodation suitable for the dispatch of business". The platforms were covered by an ornamented roof, "the whole having a chaste and imposing appearance". There were "18 up trains and 13 down daily except on Sundays when there are 5 up and 4 down".

Attention was also given to the convenience of passengers at intermediate stations. In 1840 the Chester and Birkenhead company provided a hut for the "market people" going by an early morning train from Hooton Lane Bridge to Liverpool. It also used cottages at Sutton, Mollington and Bebington. In the 1840s the Birmingham and Manchester Company was providing a passenger shed at all stations between Crewe and Stockport. They were to be constructed of "red deal with boards upright and well rabbitted". When at last the Crewe–Shrewsbury line provided Nantwich with a station ("a small neat structure but affording every convenience and need for the purpose intended"), Worleston (which had hitherto been called Nantwich) had to be renamed. Finally in 1861, it was announced with pride that Stockport (Edgeley) was to be rebuilt "with convenient waiting rooms and a new approach".

Most of the remaining stations gained no more description than that they were "neat", but their importance in the social history of the county cannot be ignored. As the engineers sought to join great towns by the shortest, practicable routes, in very many instances the railway stations of Cheshire (and of other counties) had to be built at some distance from the small towns and villages whose names they bore. The period of station-building coincided with the very extensive building operations in the growing towns of Birkenhead, Crewe, Stockport and in the new residential regions in Wirral and south of Manchester. It coincided also with the erection of very many National Schools and Nonconformist chapels and such mansions as Peckforton Castle.

No two stations were quite alike but the majority consisted of booking office, waiting room or rooms, together with some sort of shelter for the station coal, the oil and lamps and sometimes the station barrows or trucks. There might be also a room for parcels forwarded by train. Later when the electric telegraph was used there was a signal box, and if the volume of business warranted it, there was a goods yard with a covered building containing a small office or merely a desk for clerical work. At many stations there was a siding into which goods trains could be run to enable a passenger train to pass.

Farmers and well-to-do people might reach the stations in their own "traps" or other conveyances, but there were facilities for poorer folk. A very extensive service of communications with Chester was maintained by carriers from every village within a dozen miles. A similar service developed around Crewe. Poorer people travelled with the carrier or reached the railway in the buses which were found in many places. In the 1860s, for example, a bus ran each day from Macclesfield to Chelford station; and in 1845 there was a service between Knutsford and Chelford; coaches from Congleton met every train at Congleton station in the 1850s, and a good service of buses connected Runcorn with the stations at Moore. Omnibuses from Northwich met the trains at Hartford; a carrier went three days a week from Middlewich to Sandbach station;

a bus from Tattenhall met every train at Tattenhall Road station, and from Stockport there were road services to New Mills, Marple, Buxton, Chapel-en-le-Firth and Hayfield. In most parts of Cheshire travel was possible even for the poorer people—if they could afford it. In England as a whole, however, only 17 per cent of the passengers in 1845 held third-class tickets. (In 1875, it was 77 per cent and in 1911, 96 per cent.)

Though we have treated the material rather than the personal aspects of railway development in Cheshire, a brief note must be added on Thomas Brassey (1805–70) the great railway contractor of the period and himself a Cheshire man. His family farmed at Bulkeley and at Buerton; he went to school at Chester, and was articled to a land agent and surveyor and became impressed with Telford's road to Holyhead. George Stephenson advised him to try his hand at railway building.

He tendered unsuccessfully for the Dutton viaduct, but his work lies in and around Cheshire (and indeed elsewhere in England and France)—between Chester and Ruabon in the two great viaducts near Chirk, between Stafford and Wolverhampton in the Penkridge viaduct, in a section of the Grand Junction line south of Crewe, parts of the Crewe to Shrewsbury line, of the Chester and Holyhead line, of the Chester and Crewe line, the Chester and Warrington line, the Warrington to Altrincham line and the Hooton and Parkgate line. He also built Chester station.

Chapter Three

THE RAILWAYS IN OPERATION

The first train from Liverpool to Birmingham ran (through Cheshire) on 7th July 1837. A correspondent who made the journey sent a long description to the *Chester Courant*: "The carriages are superb," he wrote. "Everything in the shape of elegance is to be found in those belonging to the First Class. The Second Class carriages are of a similar construction and wholly enclosed; the only distinction being that the Second Class carriages are without linings. Mail coaches have accommodation for four passengers in each compartment." He mentioned the Bridgewater Canal under which the line passed, the view from the Dutton Viaduct, the halts at Warrington, at Hartford and at Crewe where the assembled spectators viewed the train with great interest. After a stop of eight minutes (8.57–9.05), the train sped southwards, mounted the Madeley incline but had difficulty over its water supply near Whitmore.

With commendable promptitude, the Company produced a small Railway Companion, containing a map, information about fares, regulations, train-times and places on or near the route. The journey (from Liverpool or Manchester to Birmingham) took four hours (First Class) but had been done in three and a half. Mixed trains stopped at all stations and took five and a quarter or five and a half hours. Second Class carriages were roofed but the driver and fireman had no protection against the weather nor had those passengers who preferred riding outside (that is on the roof). No smoking was allowed in any carriage—even with the consent of the other passengers; and no refreshments were on sale: they would cause delay and even accidents. Porters dealt with luggage. No gratuities were allowed.

Of the opening of the Chester and Birkenhead line, the press reported that the directors and the Mayors of Liverpool and Chester were present. A "train of enormous length" drawn by two engines left Birkenhead to the sound of cheers and the firing of cannons. "We enter the Chester Station at Brook Street where we are merely separated by a gate from the Chester and Crewe railway."

The opening of the Chester and Crewe Railway secured less publicity, but it was an "important event" for it "shortened the journey between the Mersey and the Metropolis by fifteen miles". It was understood that the mails for Ireland and those for Liverpool would proceed along this route.

The government gradually acquired a measure of control of this rapidly growing means of conveying people and goods. By Acts of 1840, 1842 and 1844, it asserted its right to inspect; to demand returns of traffic, tolls and accidents; it required covered accommodation to be provided for passengers at a charge of a penny a mile; and it compelled the companies to run at least one train a day in both directions, stopping at every station at this fare (the "parliamentary train"). Within the bounds thus set, directors enjoyed a large measure of freedom. This they used to experiment with styles of train, with fares, with frequency of service, and with attempts to attract more business.

The trains were mail, first-class, second-class and mixed. The mails were of course the fastest. First-class carriages were well upholstered; second-class had no upholstery. A third-class which had no cover had been in use, but the Chester and Birkenhead Company resolved in 1841 to have a fourth-class "as soon as practicable". In 1842, the Manchester and Birmingham Company defined its policy while fixing its fares, thus: "persons in open carriages without seats $\frac{3}{8}$d a mile; in second-class carriages with glass windows $\frac{3}{4}$d a mile; in other carriages $1\frac{1}{2}$d a mile". It had to cope with a "great and expected increase in the number of passengers availing themselves of the Cheap Trains", and when a man was thrown off a box wagon and killed as he was getting out at Alderley, it was resolved to discontinue the use of these wagons for passengers, and orders were given for ten "Third Class Passenger Carriages with Doors opening at the sides". Each carriage was to have a brake.

In the first-class carriages there were windows that could be opened and closed and later this fitting was extended to the other classes, though there were complaints that "by denying leathers to the windows or else buttons to the leathers, the windows had either to be up or down". No heat was provided till 1856 when the Great Western placed foot warmers in first-class compartments and in 1870 in second-class.

At first the porters wore a badge when at work but it soon became the practice to provide uniforms for men working in the open air. The Manchester and Birmingham Company, for example, gathered information from other companies and decided in 1843 to supply Guards, Policemen and Porters with one suit a year and Guards and Policemen with a great coat every two years. The inside staff received no clothing and may have experienced some dissatisfaction. In the same year orders were given to alter Sandbach and Chelford stations "so as to make them habitable by the clerks in charge".

Some examples of fares in the early days:
Crewe–Liverpool 1st Cl . . . 9/6; 2nd Cl . . . 7/–; Mail . . . 11/–
Crewe–Manchester 1st Cl . . . 9/6; 2nd Cl . . . 7/–; Mail . . . 11/–
Manchester–Macclesfield 1st Cl . . . 3/6; 2nd Cl . . . 2/6; 3rd Cl . . . 2/–;
Chester–Birkenhead 1st Cl . . . 3/6; 2nd Cl . . . 2/6; 3rd Cl . . . 2/–; 4th Cl . . . 1/–
Chester–Ruabon 1st Cl . . . 3/–; 2nd Cl . . . 2/6; 3rd Cl . . . 1/5
There were, however, cheap day return tickets as early as 1843 on the Manchester and Birmingham line in the form of Pleasure Excursions to Holmes Chapel, Sandbach and Crewe; and cheap tickets were available from five stations to Stockport on Fridays and to Manchester on Saturdays; and there were return tickets at one and a half times single fare between Chester and Ruabon.

For the regular traveller there were "contracts" between Macclesfield and Manchester certainly as early as 1846 and there is an acid comment on season tickets to Wilmslow and Alderley Edge in the Macclesfield Courier in January 1856: they increased the traffic . . . but were "of course, unprofitable customers", but each was the head of a family and had servants and friends. The charge for annual contracts between Chester and Birkenhead in 1847 was £15, in 1849 £18.10.0. By 1859 it was proposed to raise it to £22.10.0, but the Company grudgingly accepted a lower figure of £20.

Poor children were catered for when in 1843 the Manchester and Birmingham Company decided to convey Charity Schools and their teachers to Stockport and back for 6d, or to Alderley for 9d. Horse lovers were not disregarded; a "special" was run from Manchester to Chester via Crewe for the races in 1843. In 1844 grooms in charge of horses were allowed to travel in the horse-box free, and in 1845 when an application was received for special trains during the hunting season, it was conditionally conceded.

In the 1850s almost any event which promised business called for suitable arrangements. Of Beeston Festival the Chester Courant reported in 1852 "Trains from all parts have been announced for the convenience of visitors" and the following week "The Station Master [at Chester] afforded every comfort by his courtesy and attention". In 1856 trains from Chester and Crewe conveyed passengers to Beeston and back at a single fare. In that year, a "special train was very accommodatingly put on ... for an outing of the Mold Ladies Club by the Chester and Mold Railway Company". And in 1864 the Headmaster at Tilstone (Fearnel, 1½ miles beyond Tarporley) notes in his logbook "Below the average (attendance) on account of a Sunday Schools excursion in the neighbourhood of Rhyl".

But longer excursions were becoming possible and indeed practicable in the 1850s. For the opening of the Shrewsbury and Ludlow line (1852), a special train was run from Chester.

The North Wales line received due support. Late in 1851 the completion of the tubular bridge across the Menai Strait afforded uninterrupted connection between Holyhead and London. An article from the Morning Herald, reprinted in the Chester Courant in July 1852, praised the engineers, the speed and punctuality of the trains and gave credit to the L.N.W.R. for the support afforded to the Chester and Holyhead Railway. Before the line was opened, notice was given of two cheap excursions "to view the great breakwater now being erected ... at Holyhead besides the many and historic beauties of the locality". In 1852, a "Cheap and Select" Excursion to Bangor and the Britannia Bridge ran from Chester. The train consisted of sixteen first-class carriages, and "the lights in the carriages contributed much to the comfort of the passengers in passing through the tunnels". In the summer of 1856, an advertisement showed trains running every hour from Birkenhead to Chester for excursions to North Wales.

In 1851 the Great Exhibition held in Hyde Park led all the Railway Companies to offer transport to London at reduced fares. The L. & N.W.R. had expected a decline in traffic after the close of the Exhibition but it did not suffer. The North Stafford however was "prejudicially affected": cheap trips to London did not compensate for losses on other traffic and the Macclesfield Courier referred to "ruinously low fares". When the buildings were moved to Sydenham, there were occasional attempts to attract passengers to the Crystal Palace. In 1858 for example, there was a trip from Birkenhead and Chester (by G.W.R., of course) at fares (from Chester) of 21s first-class, 11s covered carriages; and in mid-

September the first-class fare was reduced to 18s 6d. In the same year, the Railway Times advertised seven-day cheap tickets from Paddington to Chester at 21s first-class, 11s second-class, and 28-day tickets at 37s first-class, and 17s second-class.

The Royal Agricultural Show was held at Chester in 1858. The *Courant* was full of praise for the benefits the railways had brought to farmers in general and for those running into Chester in particular. They had constructed "a siding from the main line in the Infirmary Field for the special accommodation of the Show ... Immense arrivals of heavy machinery and implements" had been unloaded there and forwarded to the Roodee. Implements had come from firms (still well known) at Ipswich, Bedford, Lincoln and Reading. Under arrangements made by the Railway Clearing House, the companies agreed to carry livestock without trans-shipment and also free to the exhibition and implements at half the usual charges.

The railways made it possible to draw large numbers of people to Chester Races. The *Courant* published a front-page advertisement in 1858 stating that "a fast special will leave the General Station, Chester, at 6.0 p.m. on 6th May for Birmingham, Leamington, Oxford and London". It supplied the number of arrivals and departures for each of the four days on which the races were held by each of the railways: the Birkenhead Railway, the Manchester and Cheshire Junction, the London and North Western, the Chester and Holyhead and the Great Western. The second day's arrivals (the Chester Cup day) was by far the largest, reaching 28,810 in 1860 and 26,550 in 1861. The total arrivals and departures were 91,912 in 1860 and 87,784 in 1861.

Enterprise went further in seeking business with Ireland. In 1858, first- and second-class tickets available for twenty-eight days were issued between 1st June and 2nd September to the Lakes of Killarney, and on 30th August of that year there was a trip from Manchester, Warrington, Birkenhead and Chester via Chester and Holyhead to Dublin, "allowing ten clear days for recreation returning any weekday, First Class, 20s, Covered Carriage 10s 6d". To what extent the public took advantage of this offer it would be difficult to determine.

Travellers of the period frequently speak of the view from the carriage window, but reading commonly passed the time. Emerson landed at Liverpool in 1847 and travelled to London (and therefore through Cheshire). "The traveller", he writes, "cushioned and comforted in every manner . . . rides as on a

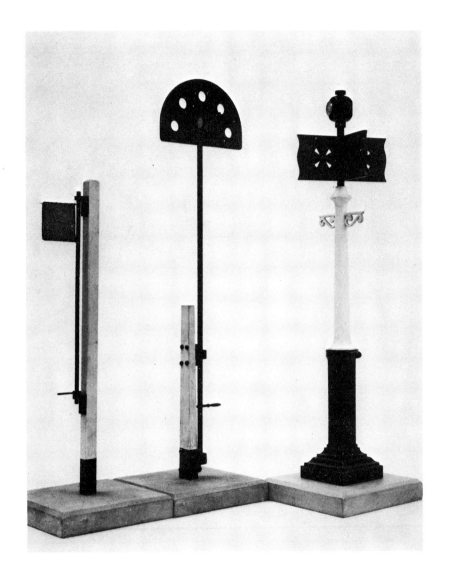

Grand Junction Railway Signals 1838

John Ramsbottom
Locomotive Superintendent of the L.N.W.R.
1846–57

Plate XXI

GOODS-LOCOMOTIVE BY ALEXANDER ALLAN. CREWE.

FOR THE

LONDON AND NORTH WESTERN RAILWAY.

NORTHERN DIVISION

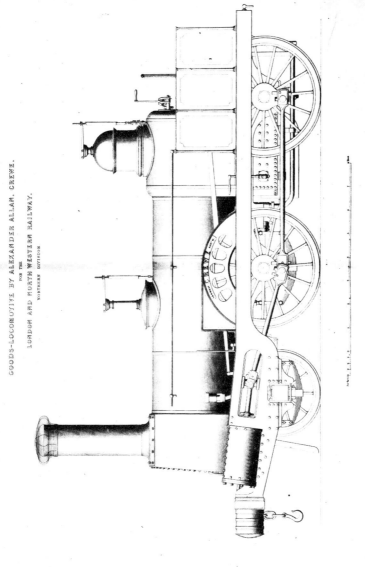

BLACKIE & SON "GLASGOW" EDINBURGH & LONDON

Goods-Locomotive, by Allan, 1851

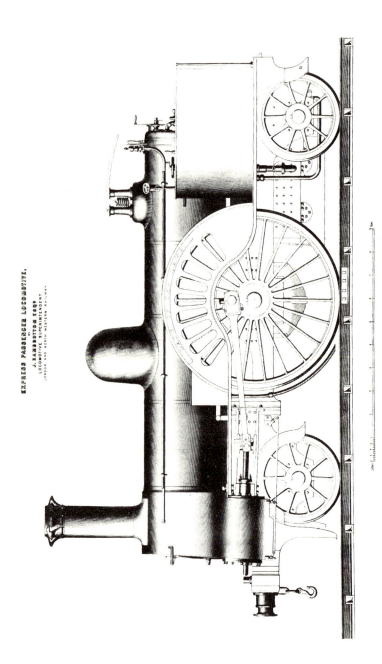

EXPRESS PASSENGER LOCOMOTIVE,
BY
J. RAMSBOTTOM ESQ?
LOCOMOTIVE SUPERINTENDENT
LONDON AND NORTH WESTERN RAILWAY

"*Lady of the Lake,*" *one of Ramsbottom's type of engine*

cannon-ball, high and low, over rivers and towns, through mountains, in tunnels of three or four miles, at near twice the speed of our (American) trains; and reads quietly the *Times* newspaper". In 1848 Messrs. W. H. Smith opened a stall for the sale of newspapers, periodicals and books on Euston station, and in the following year at Crewe, Liverpool and Manchester. In 1851, the *Courant* commented on Literature for the Rail and gave long extracts from Railway Novels or Readings for the Rail. The London morning papers reached Liverpool by 2.30 p.m., but in 1852 the *Courant* announced that the L.N.W.R. was to run a special fast train bringing them to Liverpool "and, we hope, Chester" by 12.30 p.m.

The innovation in modes of travel brought new hazards into human life. In Peacock's *Gryll Grange*, the Reverend Doctor Opimiam attributed "disasters" on the railways to the public "insanity for speed". The ladies of *Cranford* (Knutsford in Cheshire) held railways to be "obnoxious". They were deeply shocked when a half-pay captain was killed in rescuing a child from an approaching train.

Accidents of all kinds on the railways received full prominence in the press. In September 1858 the *Courant* had a leading article on "The Dangers of Railway Travelling" and in January 1861, it stated "Railway accidents are unhappily becoming the chief topic of domestic interest. . . ." The new form of transport was thoroughly established but interest in its performance remained keen. Besides, an account of an accident could be rendered lively as when a train was reported to have descended Madeley bank towards Crewe at 60 miles an hour, to have applied the brakes, reversed the engine and reduced speed to 6 miles an hour within 150 yards, and to have sent trucks of a goods train flying.

Accidents in Britain as a whole were common but accidents in mines and factories and on the roads occurred with equal frequency and some of them were equally trivial. Until the fences along each side of the railroad were well grown, cattle were bound to stray on the track; there were bound to be a few deaths due to carelessness and a few collisions owing to the fortuitous breakage of couplings. Only two serious accidents occurred in Cheshire during our period.

The first occurred on 24th May 1847, when as the 6.15 p.m. train from Chester to Wrexham was crossing the Dee bridge, the third arch broke, and the train fell into the river causing the death of five people. The incident was of course widely discussed and the Report of the Commissioners of Railways who investigated the accident, contains copious details together with six large drawings of the structure. The report does not allocate blame to anybody. (Robert Stephenson was the engineer.) It appears to answer two unspoken questions: first, what steps should be taken to prevent a similar accident? To which it offers the recommendation of research on the strength of metals. And second, how far does inspection by a government officer (before the opening of a line) guarantee the security of a structure? The answer is decisive: responsibility must rest with the railway company and their engineers. The failure of an *iron* bridge caused the Railway Department of the Board of Trade to send a questionnaire and a demand for plans of iron bridges to all the railway companies in the country.

The other serious accident occurred on the evening of the Chester Cup day, 1851, when very many passengers were returning to Manchester. A heavily loaded train departed from Chester at 7.0 p.m., followed by a second train, and at 8.0 p.m. by a third. The first train had but one engine; its pace was slow; it entered Sutton (Halton) tunnel considerably behind time and lost speed still further in the tunnel. The second train arrived, was helping to push the first, but making very slow progress and both engines lacked water. The third train came; no red light was shown at the rear of the second train; there was a crash and the tunnel was completely blocked with the debris of carriages, dead and wounded. Five people were killed and thirty or forty were seriously injured.

For fatal accidents travellers could make some provision. In 1848, the Chester newspapers carried a notice that the Railway Passengers' Assurance Company was issuing tickets at the following rates:

3d in case of death to	1st Class passengers:					£1,000
2d	,,	,,	2nd	,,	,,	£500
1d	,,	,,	3rd	,,	,,	£200

The G.P.O. and the railways were equally alert to the advantages of transport by rail. In 1836, the Grand Junction Railway Company adopted the design of a mail carriage already chosen by the London and Birmingham Railway. From Chester (before the railway reached that place), the mails were conveyed to Hartford for forwarding by rail to London. Before the line reached Holyhead, the Chester and Crewe and the Chester and Birkenhead Companies were eager to share in carrying mail bags (via Liverpool) to Dublin. Before the Britannia Bridge spanned the Menai Strait, the Irish Mail was conveyed to Bangor by rail, across Telford's bridge by road, and on to Holyhead by train. Soon the Irish Mail train became the symbol of railway efficiency. The Post Office demanded an average speed of 42 m.p.h., and in the 1860s, it was the fastest train in Great Britain. Even in the early years of the present century, there was a feeling of pride as it drew punctually— usually double-headed—into Crewe and Chester. Legend said that the railway company forfeited £1 a minute for lateness.

And the people of Cheshire were well served as may be seen in the number of trains a day stopping at some intermediate stations in 1860:

	Up	Down		Up	Down
Chesterfield–Birkenhead–– Bebington	9	9	Crewe–Manchester– Sandbach	7	7
Chester–Crewe– Beeston Castle	9	9	Crewe–Warrington– Hartford	6	8
Chester–Warrington– Frodsham	5	5	Crewe–Shrewsbury– Nantwich	"several"	
Altrincham–Manchester	17	17			

Finally, speeds were being improved. The first Grand Junction trains had made the journey between Crewe and Liverpool at a speed of 21½ miles per hour. By 1848 it was possible to travel from Chester to London in 6½ hours; by 1851 in 5 hours 35 minutes; by 1860 the 9.0 a.m. train from Euston reached Crewe in 4 hours, with connection for Chester in 4 hours 55 minutes. This represents a speed to Crewe of 39½ miles per hour.

Chapter Four

RESULTS

In the late 1830s the coach services were advertised on the front page of the *Courant*. Prominent among them was that for the Royal Mail which left Bridge Street, Chester, every morning at 10 o'clock and arrived at Charing Cross, London, at 6 o'clock the following morning (taking 20 hours). A return coach left London at 7.30 p.m. every day, reaching Chester at 4.0 p.m. the following day (taking 20½ hours). The stage was already set for a combination of services and soon for the death of the coaches. Sixteen miles away the Grand Junction trains ran from Liverpool to London, stopping at Hartford (for Northwich). To Hartford, therefore, passengers were carried in 1839 and, joining the southbound train, they reached London in 11 hours. By 1841 the opening of the line from Chester to Crewe enabled travellers to make the whole journey by first-class train in 8½ hours (with changes at Crewe and Birmingham). A few years later the Trent Valley line (between Stafford and Rugby avoiding Birmingham) shortened the time still further. As similar reductions in travelling time were made in the journeys to Shrewsbury and to Holyhead, the coaches ceased to compete; their advertisements no longer appeared on page one. Railway timetables took their place.

There were pathetic attempts to prove that the coaches could provide a comparable service if not in speed, then in amenity. One such occurred in Cheshire between Chester and Tranmere in 1849, when an ironic writer described "used-up coachmen" emerging from "obscure retreats . . . since the fiery dragons of the iron rails have snorted over their abandoned occupation". "People may laugh as they please about the folly of competition between horse-flesh and steam but in these days," he said, "a ride through a pleasant country on the box seat behind four good tits from Chester to Liverpool for a shilling or an inside snuggery for eighteen pence is not to be sneezed at. . . ."

But it was an unequal contest. Neither in speed, comfort, cost of travel or reliability could the coaches compete successfully. Early in 1852 (after less than twelve years experience of the railways), the *Courant* published an article commenting on haulage, fuel and speed. A train, it argued, of about eighty tons conveying about 240 passengers, making the journey from Liverpool to Birmingham and back (190 miles) takes 4¼ hours each way and consumes four tons of coal costing about £5. To carry the same number of passengers between the same places every day by stage coach would require 20 coaches, 3,800 horses and would take 15 hours.

In Cheshire which had borne so much through traffic, the stage coaches quickly ceased to operate. On the Liverpool journey, they had been seen every day between Newcastle and Congleton, Knutsford and Warrington; on the Holyhead route they had gone by way of Eccleshall, Nantwich, Tarporley, and Chester (though recently that route had been superseded by Telford's new road); on the journey to Manchester they had used three routes converging on Stockport, namely the roads passing through Matlock and Chapel-en-le-Frith, through Leek and Macclesfield, and through Buxton. The way from Bristol to Manchester lay through Shrewsbury, Whitchurch, Tarporley and Northwich; that from Birmingham to Manchester passed through Newcastle, Congleton and Wilmslow. On the roads made and improved by the Turnpike Trusts supplies of horses had ensured prompt relays and good speeds. The passage of a coach had marked the time of day for the labourer in the field and the cottager who had no clock. Its arrival in a village or town with the travellers, the mails and the journals had afforded the prospect of news. Hostelries, post horse stables, harness makers and blacksmiths had profited from the traffic. Their profits rapidly declined. So did those of the Turnpike Trusts.

As already stated, the first railway in the county had not been made for the purpose of serving the needs of Cheshire. Its aim had been to connect Birmingham with Liverpool and Manchester, and the route chosen neglected all three of the old salt towns of Cheshire and produced a focus of railway communications at Crewe—a place scarcely large enough to merit the name village till the Grand Junction chose it for its locomotive works. The pattern of railway communications differed from that of communication by road.

Nevertheless, the nodal aspect of Cheshire remained. Travellers from Bristol, Birmingham or London on their way to Holyhead, Liverpool, Manchester or even Glasgow had to pass through Crewe. From Nottingham and Derby to North Wales the route lay via Stoke, Crewe and Chester. And every train halted at Crewe both because of its importance as a centre of traffic and because on the longer journeys it was necessary to change engines. The Holyhead trains stopped at

Chester also and the Manchester trains at Stockport. Cheshire bore more through traffic than any county in England. And, as stated previously, its traffic began early: in 1843 when a dozen counties had no railways and in Wales railroads had hardly begun, Cheshire had practically a hundred miles of track in regular use. By the mid-century the main routes (except that from Shrewsbury to Crewe) had been laid as they remained throughout the railway era.

Building continued but it was mainly quite local. A deviation at Weaver Junction and the construction of a bridge six miles west of the original Mersey crossing shortened the line to Liverpool and provided Runcorn with a station (1869). The Wirral was opened up by short lines: Birkenhead to Hoylake (1866), Hoylake to West Kirby (1878), Birkenhead to Wallasey and New Brighton (1888), Hooton to Helsby (1863), Hooton to Parkgate (1866), Parkgate to West Kirby (1886), (the Mersey Railway 1886), Rock Ferry connected with the Mersey Railway (1891), Hawarden Bridge to Birkenhead (1896). South of Manchester the Altrincham line was extended to Knutsford (1862), to Northwich (1863), to Chester (1874). The Stockport to Altrincham line was opened in 1865. East of Manchester of several developments we may mention the lines to Marple (1865).

These additions to the railway scheme made no material change in the basic pattern. With the exception of the new line through Runcorn to Liverpool, they were all essentially suburban services, but by affording easy access to the conurbations of Birkenhead, Liverpool and Manchester from so many places in Cheshire, they affected the distribution of population in the county. They were turning a region mainly devoted to agriculture into residential areas for middle class city workers. Hoylake and West Kirby which in 1860 had no railway, enjoyed a service of twenty trains a day to Birkenhead in 1887. Neston at the same date was within forty-five minutes of Liverpool (via Hooton). From Knutsford to Manchester Central the journey took thirty-seven minutes. From Marple to Manchester Central or to London Road (Piccadilly) in 1887 one could travel in thirty-six minutes. As for Chester itself, the Cheshire Lines route to Manchester took one hour and a quarter and the London and North Western route one and a half; and of a score of trains a day between Chester and Birkenhead, the fastest took one to Liverpool (James Street) in fifty minutes, the slowest in sixty-five minutes.

In short, we notice briefly a third phase in railway develop-

L. & N.W. Railway, Crewe Station, approx. 1845

The General Railway Station.

OPENED IN 1848.

This fine erection is considered to be one of the most perfect in its arrangements of any in the kingdom ; the cost of which, together with its auxiliary buildings, exceeded £220,000. The design was by Mr. Thompson ; the Goods' Station was planned by Mr. Parker ; the building executed by Mr. Brassey ; and the whole superintended by R. L. Jones, Esq. the present manager. It was begun in August, 1847, and finished in August, 1848. The land occupied is upwards of sixty acres ; and embraces nearly eight miles of rail. The whole extent of the Passengers' Platform, from east to west, is 1,160 feet. The best view of the Station is obtained from an elevation in an open field in front, called the "Footpath to the City." The Electric Telegraph to the principal towns of the kingdom is in full operation.

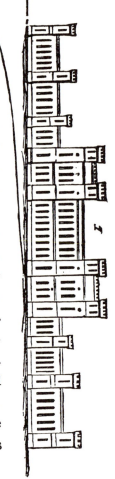

General Railway Station, Chester, (Chester Public Library)

ment. The first had been the joining of towns; the second the amalgamation of companies giving rise to a national system linking Ireland with England and England with Scotland; the third the growth of suburban services, the growth of population within the county and change in the character of the population. The phases overlapped in time but the third occurred mainly after 1860.

On three towns the railways had a material effect quite apart from trade and traffic. At Chester the Joint Committee managing the station contrived to set in motion an improvement to the dignity and convenience of the city. The station needed a better approach than that by way of Brook Street: it needed direct communication with Foregate Street. Such a road, the committee agreed, should be twelve yards wide; it would of course have to pass over the canal and that would mean raising the level of the proposed road considerably. Now the committee had no power to buy properties in Chester for the purpose of road construction, but it had an asset with which negotiations might begin: some of the land in front of the station belonged to the station site. Across this land the desired road would pass; on part of it an hotel might be built. If someone would undertake the expense of constructing the road, land for the purpose could be handed over on favourable terms.

During the summer and autumn of 1856, a Mr. Hitchin tried without success to gain the assent of owners of lands along the proposed route. Early in 1857, negotiations were opened with a group prepared to erect an hotel connected with the station by a covered way. By April, arrangements were made for the sale of 4,000 square yards of the land for the hotel and in July of that year, the deal was completed. In April 1860 the Queen Hotel was opened. The other aim took longer to achieve, but a survey was made in 1863–66; various buildings which obstructed a straight thoroughfare were demolished; the road surface over the canal was raised; and in 1866, City Road, the wide approach to the station, was opened.

At Crewe the impact of the railways was greater though it added nothing to the dignity or convenience of the town. The "works", greatly expanded from the original three and a half acres by 1848, employed more than 1,400 males. There were erecting shops capable of containing forty locomotives at a time, travelling cranes which removed locomotives from one part of a building to another, a fitting shop in which 300 men were employed, and rolling mills established to enable the company to make all their rails and chairs.

But it is important to note the growth of the town itself. In the 1850s a Mr. Thomas Stone of Newton was the principal contractor. He built the rolling mills, the pattern shop, and contracted with the railway company to build a hundred cottages of two types for £94 and £129.15s respectively. As the rolling mills progressed, he was also asked to build twenty-five cottages for the workmen employed in them.

As the railway company owned almost all the land and the houses in Crewe, and provided work for almost all the male population, a trading enterprise became committed in large measure to responsibility for the welfare of its employees. New Lanark and Saltaire have received far more attention than Crewe from social historians, but it should be recognised that the railway company took steps which only the more enlightened employers of the period deemed necessary or desirable. The company not only laid out the town and provided the houses; it provided a church, schools, baths and a Mechanics' Institute; it provided gas and water also; it even provided a banquet for the workers and their wives (1843). In short, Crewe was created by the Grand Junction and the London and North Western Railway Companies.

On Stockport the effect of the railway was regrettable, though perhaps inevitable. The town lies—the original town lay—deep in a valley. To connect it with Manchester on the one side and Alderley and Crewe on the other, it was necessary to construct a viaduct some hundred feet above the bed of the river. Built of Runcorn stone and brick, it was said to have embodied some 400,000 cubic feet of stone and 11,000,000 bricks. It was begun in March 1839 and completed late in December 1840. The twenty-two arches each of 63 feet span, four of 20 feet span and two abutments constitute a fine engineering achievement for the period, but the viaduct dominated and indeed still overshadows the whole of the original town.

✳   Though ultimately the railways played a very important part in the progress of agriculture in Cheshire, it is not possible to summarise accurately their role during the years 1840–60. Three great changes were taking place during that period, namely the use of artificial fertilisers, the use of tiles (pipes) for drainage, and the sale of liquid milk instead of cheese and butter. The changes were inter-related and con-

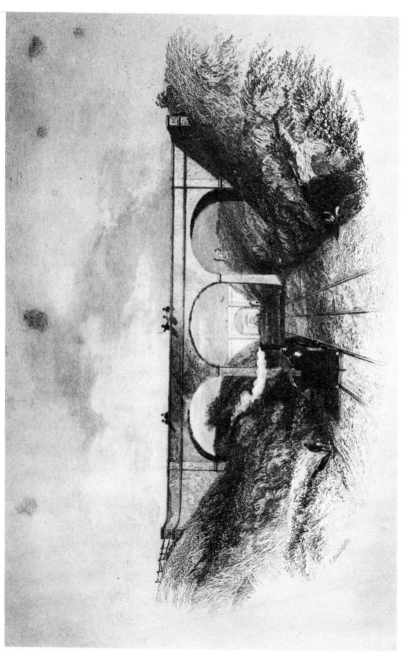

Grand Junction Railway, 1837 from "Home and Country Scenes": Excavation at Hartford

Queen Hotel, Chester, built on land bought from the Railway Company, facing the Station and City Road

ceivably all three might have taken place on one farm within a few years. But necessarily they occurred here and there over many years.

Cheshire newspapers of the period abound in advertisements for Bone Manure, Guano, Peruvian Guano, Bradbury's Guano Substitute, Sulphate of Potash, Nitrate of Soda, and Super-phosphate of Lime. The bones, boiled and finely ground, could be obtained from any town. Guano was, of course, imported. In 1845 the Manchester and Birmingham Railway included bones and manure (together with coal and salt) in its Class I of 'Rates for the Conveyance of merchandise between Manchester and Crewe'. In the same year it ordered ten wagons for the conveyance of bone dust. It is probable, however, that for some years the canals were used for carrying all kinds of fertiliser wherever they were reasonably accessible—at Winsford, for example, or Tattenhall or Beeston, though the last two were almost equally near the railway .

Very extensive work was done in draining the level pastures by the use of horse-shoe tiles and, after 1843, cylindrical tiles (or clay pipes). The Marquis of Westminster's factory produced 1,000,000 a year for his tenants, and they were made in many places where the clay was suitable. Here again, it is likely that many pipes were distributed by canal. (The Wardle tileries, for example, lay alongside the Shropshire Union canal.)

The county produced great quantities of milk but there is difficulty in obtaining evidence of its transport to Liverpool or Manchester or indeed elsewhere during that period. Medical Officers of Health have no statistics; cows were kept in towns till late in the nineteenth century; railway records tend to treat milk along with other goods as "merchandise". Nevertheless the Manchester and Birmingham Company was ordering milk trucks in 1845 and the L.N.W.R. was improving its facilities for handling traffic in milk in Liverpool in 1850. J. H. Clapham declared that in 1850 milk was supplied to Manchester and Liverpool from a distance of thirty miles around, and A. B. Mercer stated that if it was the railways which made possible the development of wholesale milk selling, it was ready money which made the turn-over from cheese-making attractive. In the north of the county, the business grew rapidly as supplies were provided for Manchester, Warrington and Stockport. By 1880 Cheshire was contributing more than 1,500,000 gallons to Liverpool's annual supply of rail-borne milk. By the end of the century the milk floats, drawn by fast horses to the railway stations, were among the stirring sights of the villages.

Cheese did not suffer in transit and large quantities hitherto sent by road or canal were now carried by rail to London and other towns. A correspondent pointed out, however, that cheese sent to London by the Great Western Railway had to be trans-shipped en route because that railway had not one continuous gauge. The Cheese Hall or Cheese Market built at Crewe in 1854 was connected by a branch to the main railway line. It was reported of the cheese fair held there in 1849, that there had been "upwards of 400 tons" of cheese "a great part of which was sold at prices varying from 40s to 50s a hundredweight".

As for other products of the farms—vegetables, fruit, eggs— these were sent to the towns by rail, but the potatoes grown extensively round Frodsham, Lymm and Altrincham, were sent to Manchester by canal.

The railways assisted the transport of live stock. Cattle had, of course, walked along the roads and lanes to market, some- times for great distances and lost a great deal of weight on the way. Now they could be transported a hundred miles in an afternoon, and thanks to the operations of the Railway Clear- ing House, they might travel to their destination in the same truck over different companies' lines. As early as 1845, the Manchester and Birmingham Company noted that this branch of traffic was growing, that they were short of trucks, and asked the London and Birmingham Company whether it could supply them with ten or twenty trucks on loan. Throughout the century Irish cattle were imported at Liver- pool and after the construction of the docks, at Birkenhead also. From Birkenhead, some of them were distributed to Chester and to Manchester by rail.

But the railways rendered a subtler service in making known the advances in agricultural machinery, implements and dairy equipment. We have noted the arrival by rail of machinery for exhibition at the Royal Agricultural Show at Chester in 1858. Special "Trials of Implements and Machinery" were staged, including steam engines and threshing machines. At a time when on many farms hand labour gathered the crop, when corn was cut by scythe or sickle, when threshing was effected by flail, when sowing was done by broadcasting seed, when turnips were split with a chopper and even the wooden plough had not entirely disappeared from the fields, the standard of farming could not be raised by pack wagon or by

canal. The products of Ipswich, Bedford and Lincoln needed
to be shown in Macclesfield, Nantwich and Chester. This the
railways achieved—not at a stroke, but by the service of
bringing the drill, the reaper, the harrow, the cheese vat . . .
to the market towns of Cheshire. Thus they made possible a
readier acceptance of new ideas and inventions.

Before the railway era, coal had been distributed by the
canals and often carried long distances by cart. In west Cheshire, supplies were drawn almost entirely from North Wales,
in east Cheshire from Lord Vernon's collieries at Poynton and
from mines in the industrial north-east of the county. The
railways, as had been foreseen, made the carriage cheaper and
faster. In 1846, the Chester and Holyhead Railway reached
Saltney and the Shrewsbury and Chester Company extended
via Saltney to Ruabon in the same year. This opened railway
communication between the coalfield around Wrexham and
Chester. In a book published in 1848, it was pointed out that
whereas coal sent from Wrexham to Chester had had to be
conveyed by canal barge via Whitchurch and Nantwich at a
cost of 15s to 18s a ton or (in necessarily small quantities) by
cart 12 or 16 miles, it was now taken a mere 12 miles by rail
and the cost was 7s 6d a ton. In 1860 the Brymbo Coal, the
Bryn Malley Coal and Coke and the Coed Talon Coal
Companies had agencies in Chester, but coal for gas produc-
tion came from Lancashire. Brymbo Coal was also on sale in
Birkenhead together with coal from Haydock collieries near
Warrington. Crewe drew its supplies from Haydock and from
Poynton.

In the east, the Manchester and Birmingham Company
had its wharves at each station between Stockport and Crewe
in the middle 1840s, and an entry in its books shows the
Company contriving to oblige a dealer (who provided his
own wagons) by delivering coal in Crewe at a charge of $1\frac{1}{2}$d
per ton per mile.

Still further east (where there was no navigable waterway
till the opening of the Macclesfield canal in 1830), Lord Vernon took the earliest opportunity of using the railways. The
first part of the Cheadle Hulme to Macclesfield branch
(opened in 1845) ran to Prince Pit, Poynton. The second part
was built from a point near the present station to Macclesfield,
leaving the colliery line as a "branch off a branch". Along
this subsidiary, Lord Vernon's coal was conveyed to Stockport,
Crewe and elsewhere. He surrendered to the railway company

all the wharves he held and entered into a new agreement for wharfage on all coals or slack delivered after 1st January 1848 to any wharf on or adjacent to the L.N.W.R.

An interesting statement on the coal traffic appeared in the Report of the General Manager of the Birkenhead Railway Company in March 1860. Receipts for transport of coal had risen between 1856 and 1859 from £13,693 to £22,614. Coal from Lancashire was used in households and for furnaces and for gasworks; coal from Wales for export. He quoted the weight of coal derived from each source and went on to make his recommendations. Concerning the home trade, water-borne coal had ceased but the company had made no special accommodation for it. It was a "growing and remunerative traffic of great importance", needing coal yards, sidings and offices. As for the export trade, there was a "great opening". It needed "mechanical means of shipment", the Company must get "complete and convenient access for the trucks to all the quays as well as the most approved and modern appliances for the expeditious and economical transfer of merchandise between the railway wagons and the vessels in the docks. . . ."

He went beyond his company's railway: there was a need for through trains, he said, that is through Chester which "should not be a costly terminus for all the lines but a simple junction affording facilities for quick transit". The management at Chester were studying "how much work could be done there instead of how little".

On the postal service the railway had a great effect. A "penny post" was in existence in the 1830s from Manchester to Hyde, Ashton-under-Lyne and Stalybridge by coach; to Altrincham, Cheadle and Wilmslow by Horse Post. But the charges for transmission of letters from London were, of course, greater. In the late 1830s, the charge for deliveries to Congleton, Macclesfield and Nantwich had been 10d, to Chester and most other places in the county, 11d. The introduction of the universal penny post in 1840, coinciding with the early days of the railways gave a great impetus to correspondence.

The use of the Travelling Post Office and of the devices for dropping and picking up mail bags without halting the train, enabled letters to reach scores of places remote from the old coach routes (and indeed from the new railways) every day. Letters arrived twice a day at Birkenhead, Liscard, Egremont, New Brighton and Wallasey, at Chester, Runcorn,

Altrincham, Nantwich and Macclesfield. By the 1850s post offices were to be found in almost every considerable village in Cheshire—commonly, of course, housed with a retail business. Street pillar boxes were provided after 1854.

The distribution followed the lines that might have been expected. From Chester, the bags were taken along the Dee valley to places between Farndon in the south and Neston and Parkgate on the estuary; while West Kirby received letters via Birkenhead. Cheadle was served from Manchester, Cheadle Hulme from Stockport. From Congleton letters were distributed to Chelford, Capesthorne and Astbury. Nantwich was a centre of distribution for places as far away as Tarporley. Runcorn had, of course, a post office but the mail bags had to be brought from the station at Moore to which omnibuses ran several times a day. By 1860 Macclesfield Post Office was dealing with 500,000 letters a year.

Within twenty years a vast transformation had been effected in the economic life of Cheshire. The stage coach had been superseded by the train, the road by the rail, the series of horse-drawn wagons by the goods train. And communications in general had been greatly improved. A journey to the capital no longer called for fortitude to ensure a day and a night's travel: it could be accomplished in five hours. Every village had its daily delivery of letters; the towns had two deliveries; Birkenhead had three. The London newspapers reached the town on the day of publication. Agricultural progress was accelerated by displays of superior machines in the towns, at the fairs and shows. Cattle and cheese could be swiftly transported by train and Manchester and Liverpool were beginning to be supplied with milk from Cheshire. It was from the coal wharf at the railway station and not from the canal side that the merchant was distributing his coal.

A new industry, that of engine building and repairing with the ancillary industry of rail-making, had been planted in Cheshire; a new town built; a new centre of communication created. The industry grew; the town prospered; the communications advanced in importance.

That these advantages came early in Cheshire was due, as we have emphasised, to its location on the natural highway to Lancashire and the North on the one hand, to Ireland on the other hand; and a century later when electricity superseded steam power, the first electrically-hauled trains ran through Cheshire.

ROYAL HOTEL, CHESTER.

ROYAL MAIL, AND UNIVERSAL COACH OFFICE, AND

RAILWAY BOOKING OFFICE.

MESSRS. JONES AND HERBERT,

Appointed Agents to the GRAND JUNCTION, BIRMINGHAM, COVENTRY, LONDON, KIDDERMINSTER, WORCESTER, CHELTENHAM, GLOUCESTER, BATH AND BRISTOL; also the BIRKENHEAD, LIVERPOOL, MANCHESTER, LEEDS, YORK, SELBY, HULL, DERBY, AND NOTTINGHAM RAILWAY COMPANIES.

MESSRS. JONES and HERBERT respectfully beg leave to acquaint the Nobility, Gentry, Bankers, Merchants, Solicitors, Tradesmen, and others of the city of Chester and the neighbourhood, and also the different towns in the Principality, that they receive and book at their Office, the Royal Hotel, passengers, parcels, and luggage, and convey the same to the Railway Stations, Brook-street, by Omnibus, and the different Royal Mails and Coaches to meet every Train connected with the above lines of Railway.

Passengers, Parcels, and Goods booked by Messrs. HORNE and CHAPLAIN, Agents to the Grand Junction Company, London; and Messrs. WARDLE and BRETHERTON, Birmingham, through to Chester, Bangor, Carnarvon, and Holyhead, and the different towns in North and South Wales, by the following royal Mails and Post Coaches :—

Passengers and Parcels for Messrs. JONES and HERBERT'S Mails and Coaches, booked at the Railway Offices, Top Corner of James's-street, Liverpool.

The following ROYAL MAILS, and WELL-REGULATED COACHES, depart from, and arrive at, the above Office daily :—

Passengers from Liverpool by the eight o'clock Train meet the L'HIRONDELLE Coach through Wrexham, Overton, Ellesmere, Cockshut, Shrewsbury, Ironbridge Bridgnorth, Kidderminster, Worcester, Tewkesbury, Cheltenham, Gloucester, &c.—and the NETTLE through Wrexham, Ruabon, Chirk, Oswestry, Llanermynech, Welshpool, Newtown, Aberystwith, &c.

The Train leaving Birkenhead at ten minutes before one o'clock, meets the LIVER Coach through Hanley, Broxton, Malpas, Whitchurch, Wem, Salop,—and the NETTLE through Wrexham, Ruabon, Chirk, and Oswestry.

The Train leaving Birkenhead at four o'clock, meets the SWALLOW, through Pulford, Gresford, Wrexham, Ruabon, Llangollen, &c.,—and the ROYAL MAIL, through Hawarden, Northop, Holywell, St. Asaph, Abergele, Conway, Aber, Bangor, Mona, to Holyhead, from whence the Government Steam packet sails for Dublin.

Passengers for Liverpool are conveyed from the Royal Hotel Coach Office, to the RAILWAY STATION, at the following hours :—
Morning, 5—7—9—10—12 ; Evening, 2—4—6—8.
And for the Grand Junction Railway Trains, at the following hours :—Morning, 4—11 ; Evening, 4½—7½.

Chester Courant *14th June 1842*

ACKNOWLEDGMENTS

ILLUSTRATIONS

Crown Copyright.   Science Museum.

Page 33   Chester Station, 1840 (216/46)
Page 43   Model of Grand Junction Railway Signals (356)

Photographs, Science Museum Collection

Page 6   Joseph Locke, 112/37
Page 19   Warrington Viaduct, 185/46
Page 23   Dutton Viaduct, 187/46
Page 44   J. Ramsbottom, 3680
Page 45   Goods Locomotive, Allen, 813/56
Page 46   Lady of the Lake, 483/53
Page 57   Excavations at Hartford, 182/46

CHESHIRE—Crutchley's Map

It can be dated from the fact that it does not show Cheshire Lines Railway nor Crewe to Shrewsbury Railway nor line through Runcorn. It is marred by showing railways and canals too much alike